Foreword

The Submissive Activity Book is your ticket to self-accountability during your journey as a submissive in the Leather and BDSM Communities. This book contains exercises and recommendations to help you improve your service with or without a power exchange relationship. If you've ever felt disconnected from your service because you weren't actively serving a dominant, this book is for you. When you learn to be accountable to yourself, you'll find serving others easier and more fulfilling. If you're engaged in a power exchange relationship and want to improve your service, this book is the perfect tool to use in conjunction with your dominant. Together you can improve your service to meet their needs.

Why This Book?

Why This Book

Why This Book?

If you've picked up this book, you likely identify as a submissive in the BDSM and Leather communities. You may or may not be involved in a power exchange relationship at this time, but being part of such a relationship is a priority in your life. You recognize there are parts of your life that could be improved if you wish to make yourself more desirable to a dominant and you are ready to take the steps necessary to get started.

Perhaps you are a dominant seeking out ways to help your submissive improve his or her life. Maybe you're looking for some structured way to help them serve you better.

When I launched on the journey of creating this book, I did so with a particular group of people in mind. I admit it was the unattached submissive who it seemed would benefit most from a book like this. So often I hear these men and women lament the lack of order, structure, and accountability in their lives because they are not currently engaged in a power exchange relationship. This book is written for them, to give them the structure they crave, while teaching them to be accountable to themselves before they attempt to be accountable to anyone else.

Whether you are a submissive or a dominant, the purpose of this book is the same. I have designed this workbook to help submissives structure their lives, both leather and vanilla, and to help them improve their skills to make them more desirable to themselves and to those they might serve. Many of the activities in this book are worded in such a way to be applicable to BDSM priorities, but there is no reason why they cannot be applied to your vanilla life as well.

I recommend starting at the beginning of the book and working through the exercises as they are organized. If, however, you have a particular priority in your life you wish to address, completing the activities out of order will be no problem.

It is my sincere hope that this book will be a guide to helping submissive men and women learn to be self-sufficient and proactive in their submission. If you have any questions or comments for me regarding this book, I do hope you will contact me at sharimalin@gmail.com .

Why Learn New Skills?

Why Learn New Skills

Learning New Skills

You will probably hear a dominant or two lament, "These submissives just don't know how to do anything. They expect me to teach them everything." I know I have heard this topic come up when I've eavesdropped on dominants. You may also hear submissives say they are afraid to learn new skills because they don't know what their future dominant might want them to know. I say this: learn everything you can, whenever the opportunity presents itself. You'll never hear a dominant lament that their submissive knows how to do too many things.

The more skill sets you have when you enter into a power exchange relationship, the more tasks you can complete for and with your owner. It is a selling point, for submissives and job applicants of any type, to be able to list the jobs they have experience with. Granted the job experience you list for a power exchange relationship may be different than those you might list for a vanilla job, but the concept is the same. The more you know, the more you can do, the more marketable you are. Remember I have already said that if you wish to attract excellence, you must demonstrate excellence. What better way to demonstrate excellence than through a demonstration of your skill sets?

It is also important to continue to learn new skills because doing so will expand your horizons, both in the leather and vanilla worlds. Say you wish to learn to give manicures and pedicures. Perhaps after learning the skill, you find you wish to now work in that field. Learning the skill in a certified school will open that opportunity to you in the vanilla world while giving you a very marketable skill in the leather world.

Education does amazing things for people. It opens doors and allows you to journey down paths you may not have realized existed. The exercises in this book will help you focus your desires on skills you wish to learn while helping you develop a plan to accomplish you goals.

Needs, Wants, and Expectations

Needs Wants and Expectations

It is extremely important for you to clearly define and articulate your needs, wants, and expectations prior to engaging in a power exchange relationship, or any other relationship for that matter. Taking time to do so now, rather than waiting until you are engaged in a power exchange relationship will help head off disappointments on both sides of the relationship.

Definitions

It is important to begin with a clear understanding of what a need, a want and an expectation is. If you are not defining these terms the same as your potential partner, you're beginning your negotiation on unsteady ground.

Need

A need is something you must have to be happy and healthy in body, mind and spirit. Needs are the deal breakers of most relationships. Failure on the part of either member of a relationship to meet the needs of their partner can, and likely should, end the relationship.

Humans have basic needs such as food, water and shelter. Humans also need other things to survive. As you assess your needs, don't forget to consider your sexual and emotional needs. You may not think so now, but failure to have those kinds of needs met can be as destructive as failing to eat or drink.

Wants

Wants are those things we prefer and enjoy. When you look at your life, what things do you have that you like but could easily live without? Those are your wants.

While wants or preferences are generally more negotiable than needs, having at least some of them fulfilled will make your relationship more pleasurable and happy. I know that those of us who identify as submissive often feel as though our wants and preferences should not play any part in a power exchange relationship, I can tell you from personal experience that engaging in a relationship where your wants are never met will likely leave you miserable.

Certainly, there will be times when your wants take a back seat to those of the one you serve. However, being able to articulate your wants clearly will help your owner meet them, and you should expect a certain number of your wants and preferences to be met throughout the course of your relationship.

Expectations

At some point you may have been told, or come to believe on your own, that the submissive should have no expectations when entering into a power exchange relationship. That is simply not true. Expectations are those things we assume will be part of a relationship based on our wants and needs. If we aren't clear about what we expect from a relationship, how can we expect our partner to meet our needs or grant our wants?

You can, and should, have expectations regarding any relationship in which you engage. The key is to be clear with your partner about your expectations.

Why Examine Your Needs, Wants and Expectations

There are many reasons why you might wish to examine your needs, wants and expectations. Perhaps you are working on self-assessment. Maybe you are preparing to negotiate a relationship or a job promotion. Whatever your reasons, know that taking the time to complete this exercise will make your ultimate goals more attainable, be they relationship or career or other goals.

Communication of Needs, Wants and Expectations

While I am an advocate of simple, straight forward language, especially in relationships and negotiations, I do want to address methods of communication of your needs, wants and expectations that might be more successful than others.

I recommend, as part of this exercise, tempering your statements of needs, wants and expectations. There is an enormous difference between demanding something and asking for something. That difference can sometimes mean the difference between the continuation or ending of negotiations.

For example, one of the needs I expressed to the owner prior to our relationship was the need to know if others are brought into the relationship. This need was expressed thus: "Should you choose to make another person a full-time part of your life, please just let me know."
This request is non-confrontational and does not place any conditions on the owner. Nor does such a request represent controlling behavior on my part. It is, simply, a request. It is phrased in such a way, and contained in a context such, that the owner understands this is a need of mine. It is a requirement for my emotional health that I am aware of others in his life and what their relationship with him constitutes. He agreed to this need and has always told me about the others he plays with and with whom he engages in relationships.

Phrasing your needs and expectations in a non-confrontational way will help your partner understand them without feeling defensive. When we demand rather than request, we set ourselves up for failure because when our partner becomes defensive, he or she is unlikely to acquiesce to our needs.

Wants, Needs, and Expectations Worksheet

Name: _____ Date: _____

Wants, Needs and Expectations

Consider what you want, need, and expect in a relationship. Write it down and don't settle for anything less.

Want=Would be Nice
Need=Without this, the relationship is over
Expectation=those things we assume will be part of a relationship based on our wants and needs

I want this from a relationship

I need this from a relationship

I expect to have in this relationship

Creating a Protocol

Creating Protocol

Creating Personal Protocol

A refrain I hear often from submissive men and women who are not engaged in power exchange relationships is that they feel untethered and unaccountable. In other words, they find it difficult to maintain their station as submissive if they are not actively serving a dominant. My suggestion to them has been to create a personal protocol to be accountable to themselves.

A personal protocol serves several purposes. It gives a submissive structure and expectations to live by. It allows them the comfort of their station while they interact with the community. The use of a personal protocol also demonstrates to prospective dominant partners a submissive's dedication to their station.

No submissive man or woman I've ever spoken to has ever claimed to want to engage in a power exchange relationship with a schlub who didn't know their elbow from their knee. Instead, I always hear that these men and women seek out the best dominants in their area of desire. The best possible way to attract excellence is to be excellent. Creating and abiding by a personal protocol is a definite step in the direction of excellence. Your dedication to yourself and your station will be obvious to prospective partners when you share your personal protocol with them.

What is Protocol

It is important that we begin this exercise with a single foundation of understanding. To that end, I will define protocol as a set of rules, situationally driven, which may or may not include ritual*. This means that your personal protocol should take into account not only the behaviors you wish to encourage or discourage, but also the environment in which it is appropriate to enact those behaviors.

For example, many couples have a protocol in which the submissive is expected to remain nude while in the presence of the dominant. There is absolutely nothing wrong with having such a protocol so long as the submissive is permitted to wear clothing in situations where nudity is inappropriate.

I will recommend at this point that if you are developing a personal protocol outside of a power exchange relationship, you may want to avoid adding elements of ritual or etiquette to your protocol in order to leave those decisions to a future partner. Protocol addresses behavior, not the manner in which the behavior is enacted. Ritual and etiquette address the manner and those expectations are likely to be very personal for each dominant you might serve.

Steps to Creating a Personal Protocol

The process of creating a personal protocol is not as complicated as you might think. For the purpose of this book, I'm going to use four steps to create a personal protocol. I have previously published a workbook for creating a personal protocol that you might want to look at if you feel you need more in-depth directions.

The four steps to creating personal protocol are:

1. Describe Behaviors to Emulate and Avoid
2. Categorize and Prioritize Behaviors
3. Translate Behaviors into Directives
4. Define Consequences

Describe Behaviors to Emulate and Avoid

If you've spent any time at leather events, I'm certain you have seen a broad spectrum of behaviors enacted by submissives. I recommend taking some time to observe those submissives you admire, as well as those who set your fur on edge, so you can get a good idea of the behaviors you will want to include in your protocol.

Start with positive behaviors you wish to emulate. If you see a submissive perform a service or speak in a certain manner that you find attractive, add that behavior or speech mode to your list of behaviors. I recommend beginning with the positive behaviors because I feel it is far easier to be what you want to be than it is to avoid what you don't want. Plus, humans (and especially submissives) respond most effectively to positive reinforcement of behaviors. Additionally, it is far easier to define what you want to be than it is to explain what you don't want to be.

Once you've observed positive behaviors to emulate, you will want to observe and note negative behaviors you will want to avoid. If you notice a submissive at an event behaving in a way that makes you want to run away, note the behavior and then analyze why you are uncomfortable with the behavior. The analysis is important because you will want to determine if it is the behavior or the individual that makes you uncomfortable. For example, most bratty behavior makes my skin crawl. I feel uncomfortable because most times when I have observed bratty behavior in another submissive I have also observed the discomfort of the dominant associated with that submissive. Since my style of service involves maintaining a certain level of comfort for those I serve, I would avoid bratty behavior because it negatively affects the comfort of those I serve.

I recommend spending significant time analyzing behaviors for this portion of the exercise. The more behaviors you observe, the more comprehensive your protocol will be in the end. I also recommend phrasing your behaviors as broadly as possible. For example, you may observe a submissive who uses third person speech patterns. You might find that speech mode appealing. You could then include "Use third person speech mode" as a behavior rather than "Speak of yourself as 'this girl' when speaking to Thomas." The first statement is broad and allows for personalization of the behavior. The second statement is very specific and you may find it to be too limiting in the future.

Categorizing and Prioritizing Behaviors

Once you have made your lists of behaviors to emulate and avoid, it is time to organize your lists. I am going to recommend two steps to the organization process.

The first step is to group the behaviors together under categories. For example, you may have listed several behaviors that address issues of speech and several more that address issues of dress. Your categories, then, would be speech and dress.

Remember that in order to be effective, categories must be created so that you never have an instance where a behavior would end up in more than one category. Should you find this happening, create another category for that behavior.

Some of the most common categories for protocols include speech, dress, and demeanor. I am sure you will have behaviors that fit into those categories on your lists.

Once you have grouped all of your behaviors under their respective categories, it is time to prioritize your behaviors. Begin by numbering the most important behavior in each category as 1 and moving through the list until you have numbered each behavior based on how important you feel that behavior is to your protocol.

Prioritizing your behaviors is an important step in the process of creating a personal protocol because it allows you to cull those behaviors you don't find to be as important while emphasizing those you do. When you are finished creating your protocol, you will want it to be usable. A list of 100 more behaviors isn't going to be very useful because you are unlikely to remember all of them. Instead, a list of 20 very focused behaviors will stand you in better stead.

Take your time with this step. You will probably want to group and prioritize your behaviors and then let the lists sit for a day or two. When you return, reevaluate your prioritization to be certain you still feel they are valid. The exercises in this book are not meant to be a race. Rather taking time for reflection is a part of nearly everything we do here.

I've included a simple worksheet to help you categorize and prioritize your behaviors in this text. I've left two spaces clear of names so you can create your own categories and left space for you to use your prioritizing on the same worksheet.

Translating Behaviors into Directives

The next step in creating your personal protocol is more a grammar lesson than anything else. I know it's the English teacher in me, but it is important to rephrase each of your behaviors into directives. In technical terms, you are changing the statement of behaviors from descriptive to directive.

For example, you might have listed use respectful tone when addressing dominants as a behavior on your list. The translation of that descriptive statement to a directive might read, "The submissive will use a respectful tone when addressing dominants." Do you notice the difference? You've taken a description of a behavior you want to emulate and turned it into a directive you can follow.

The shift in phrasing is important because a protocol is a list of rules. Rules are meant to be followed and it is much easier to follow a directive than it is to interpret a description.

Define Consequences

The last step in creating your personal protocol is to define the consequences of failure to abide by protocol. It is important to know what will happen if you do not stick to your protocol, especially since you are going to have to hold yourself accountable to your protocol. It is in defining consequences for breaking protocol that you will see the importance of prioritizing your protocols as well. You will likely wish to categorize your consequences in terms of minor infractions, mid-level infractions and major infractions. The priority you placed on the protocol in step two of this exercise should help you determine where in the continuum a break in protocol should fall.

Some commonly used consequences for breaking protocol include writing essays or journal entries, researching topics related to the protocol, and creating a formal apology. You will want to decide on your own consequences, of course. I caution you only to make certain the consequence is appropriate to the breach in protocol so that when it is enacted, the consequence serves the purpose of reinforcing the usefulness of the protocol.

Remember that you are going to have to hold yourself accountable to your protocol. Until and unless you are involved in a power exchange relationship, no one else is going to punish you for breaches in protocol. However, if you wish to ensure that the hard work you've done to create this personal protocol doesn't go to waste, you are going to have to ensure you engage in the consequence behaviors you set forth in this step should you breach your protocol.

I hope that when you complete this section, you have a personal protocol you can live with and that will bring honor to your service. The purpose of a protocol is to provide structure for a submissive whether a dominant is present or not. Your personal protocol should do that and at such times when you are engaged in a power exchange relationship, you will be able to share your personal protocol with your partner. They will likely be impressed that you have taken the time to complete this exercise and you know they are already impressed with your ability to abide by your personal protocol. Very likely it is your adherence to your protocol that has brought you to the attention of your partner in the first place.

Behaviors to Emulate or Avoid

Behaviors to Emulate and Avoid

Name

Date

For this Exercise, use the top right and left boxes to write down the behaviors you want to emulate and avoid.

In the second row, add the why behind your desire to either emulate or avoid those behaviors.

Behaviors to Emulate	Behaviors to Avoid
Why Emulate these Behaviors?	Why Avoid these Behaviors?

Categorize and Prioritize Behaviors

Categorized Behaviors

SPEECH

BEHAVIOR

DRESS

INTERACTION

NAME: DATE:

Translating Behaviors into Directives

Use this page to rewrite your behaviors as directives.

For example, if you want to emulate the behavior of kneeling beside your partner at public events, you would write that protocol as follows:

Submissive will kneel at the Dominant's right side when they are together in an appropriate, public setting.

Be specific and realistic in your protocol directive statements.

Consequences--Speech

Use these pages to clearly define and record the consequences of failure to mee the protocols you've set up with yourself and/or your dominant

I have separated these consequences by category, since it's likely different categories will carry different consequences

SPEECH

Consequences--Behavior

Use these pages to clearly define and record the consequences of failure to mee the protocols you've set up with yourself and/or your dominant.

I have separated these consequences by category, since it's likely different categories will carry different consequences

BEHAVIOR

Consequences--Dress

Use these pages to clearly define and record the consequences of failure to mee the protocols you've set up with yourself and/or your dominant

I have separated these consequences by category, since it's likely different categories will carry different consequences.

DRESS

Consequences--Interaction

Use these pages to clearly define and record the consequences of failure to mee the protocols you've set up with yourself, and/or your dominant.

I have separated these consequences by category, since it's likely different categories will carry different consequences

INTERACTION

Consequences--Other

Use these pages to clearly define and record the consequences of failure to mee the protocols you've set up with yourself and/or your dominant

I have separated these consequences by category, since it's likely different categories will carry different consequences

OTHER _____

Consequences--Other

Use these pages to clearly define and record the consequences of failure to mee the protocols you've set up with yourself and/or your dominant.

I have separated these consequences by category, since it's likely different categories will carry different consequences

OTHER _____

Full Listing of Protocols and Consequences with Signature Blocks

Full Protocol and Consequences

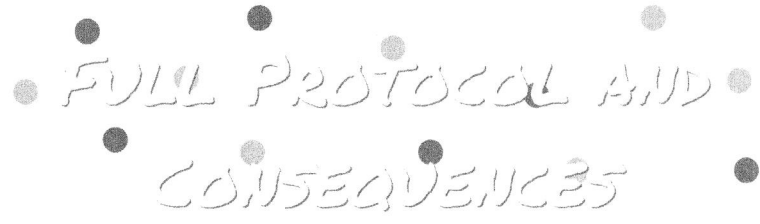

DOMINANT NAME: **SUBMISSIVE NAME:**

DATE EFFECTIVE:

Dress Protocols and Consequences

Speech Protocols and Consequences

Interaction Protocols and Consequences

Behavior Protocols and Consequences

Other Protocols and Consequences

Dominant Signature

Submissive Signature

Goal-Setting

Setting Goals

Setting Goals

This section of the activity book is designed with training as well as personal goals in mind. Should the submissive not be involved in a power-exchange relationship, there is no reason why they cannot use it for their own purposes. If and when you are engaged in a power exchange relationship, this section of the activity book is one you may wish to share with your dominant.

I've included in this book, a monthly goal tracker for you to use for the year. You can also list goals on the individual monthly calendars.

Areas of Your Life to Set Goals For

Training and Service: What do you want to accomplish to improve your knowledge and skills for those you serve?
Family and Home: What do you want to accomplish for your family and home?
Financial and Career: What do you want to accomplish to improve your financial status or career?
Spiritual and Ethical: What do you want to accomplish to improve your spiritual and ethical self?
Physical and Health: What do you want to accomplish to improve your physical self?
Social and Cultural: What do you want to accomplish in your community?
Mental and Educational: What do you want to accomplish to improve your overall knowledge?

Time Frames

It's important for you to determine the time frame in which you feel you can realistically accomplish your new goals. You can choose from the list below or create your own time frames.

Goals to accomplish in 30 Days
Goals to accomplish in 60 Days

Goals to accomplish in 90 Days
Goals to accomplish in 120 Days
Goals to accomplish in 6 months
Goals to accomplish in 12 months
Goals to accomplish in 5 years
Lifetime Goals

Writing Out Your Goals

It's important for you to understand that goals have very specific formats and should follow a plan of action in creating them. Doing these two things will help you create goals that are attainable within reasonable time frames rather than leaving you frustrated by an inability to get started on your goals.

SMART Goals

Goals should be Specific, Measurable, Attainable, Realistic and Timely.
Specific: When you write down your goals, be as specific as possible. Don't just say you want to learn new skills, list the new skills you want to learn.
Measurable: In order to achieve a goal, you have to be able to measure your success. Perhaps your goal is to learn to set a formal table. Make sure to include a test of your success (such as hosting a formal dinner) to demonstrate mastery of your goal. Choosing criteria for success will help you make your goals measurable.
Attainable: Goals should challenge you and require a strong commitment, but they should still be within the realm of possibility. The criteria you develop for the measurability of your goal will help you determine if your goal is attainable.
Realistic: A goal should be realistic so that it is attainable. Set your goals high enough so it is satisfactory to meet them but keep in mind those things that simply cannot be done. If you know, for example, that it will take a year to reach an education goal, setting it within a 6 month time frame is not realistic.
Timely: Create a clear target for achievement. If you don't give yourself a deadline, the goal is likely never to be attained.

Phrasing Goals

Use positive language: Phrase your goal statements in terms of what you can do as opposed to what you won't do.
Use details: Include specific details in your goal statement which reflect your measurable criteria.

Set rewards for meeting your goals.

Prioritize Goals

Review your goals and decide which are priorities for the specified time frame.
Once you've set high priorities for goals, focus on only a few during each month, moving from highest to lowest priority.

Create a Plan

Once you've stated your goals, determine how you intend to meet them. Make a list of all necessary steps and prioritize them.
Make sure your plan is broken down into small, attainable pieces so you stay motivated.

Share Your Goals

After you have set your goals and developed a plan for meeting them, share your goals with the one(s) you serve or others. Sharing goals helps in several ways. First, sharing your goal with those you serve will help set up motivation and accountability. Second, sharing your goals with others opens up avenues of assistance. No one said you have to reach your goals on your own. Others may have advice and help to offer to you that you won't know about if you don't share your goals.

Track Your Progress

Keep track of milestones in your plan and write them down. You'll be able to see your progress and stay motivated if you keep track of your progress toward your goals.

Review Your Month

At the end of each month, review your progress toward your goals. Determine where changes in priorities must be made and celebrate goals you have achieved. Be sure to include how you will reward yourself for meeting goals in your planning process. Rework and rewrite ongoing goals to reflect the progress you have made.

This is an excellent activity to share with the dominant in your life. You may find they're more excited about your success than even you are.

Nikitina, A. SMART goal setting. from Goal Setting Guide Web site: http://www.goal-setting-guide.com/smart-goals.html

Monthly Goal Tracker

Monthly Goals

JANUARY	FEBRUARY	MARCH

APRIL	MAY	JUNE

JULY	AUGUST	SEPTEMBER

OCTOBER	NOVEMBER	DECEMBER

Getting Your Finances in Order

Getting Finances in Order

Why Settle Your Finances

There are many reasons why it is a good idea to get your finances in order prior to engaging in a power exchange relationship. There are both personal and lifestyle reasons why this section of the activity book is important to your progress.

Personal Reasons

It is always a good idea to know where you spend your money. If you've ever reached the end of a pay period and wondered why your bank account is empty, you know the value of budgeting and keeping track of where you spend.

Knowing where you spend your money can help you save or reduce your debts. Perhaps one or more of the goals you set in an earlier chapter of this book involved saving for a particular purchase or purpose or reducing your debt. The best way to work toward those types of personal goals is to get a handle on your finances.

Lifestyle Reasons

Believe it or not, your future owner will appreciate you and your service more if you have already straightened out all areas of your life, including finances, before you enter their service. Having a handle on your personal finances demonstrates your level of personal responsibility to a prospective owner and makes you a more valuable servant.

Some owners require their servants to provide proof of their financial stability prior to engaging in a power exchange relationship. Jack Rinella, a community author and lifestyle leatherman, makes no bones about his requirement that all serious applicants wishing to serve him must be able to demonstrate to him that they are financially stable. He doesn't do this to pry into the private lives of people not yet in his service. Rather, Jack insists his servants be financially stable because he knows, realistically, he cannot afford to support these servants should they come to him with nothing. Such an assessment of both the owner and the servant is both fair and realistic. Neither member of a power exchange relationship should expect the other to be willing or able to take up full financial responsibility for them.

Another good reason to have a good idea of what your finances look like, and to make changes to improve them, is that doing so makes relocation easier. Perhaps you are looking to move to be closer to those you serve. Maybe you need to move for a personal reason. Whatever the reason for relocation, moving is expensive and often takes significant savings to accomplish without major hardship. If you don't have savings and have no idea where your finances stand, how can you honestly say to a prospective owner or employer that you can move to meet their needs?

No matter what your reasons for wanting to get your finances in order, the exercises in this chapter will help you get started in the right direction.

Creating a Budget

There are many budgeting worksheets available online and I've included one in this chapter for you to use. However, you may want to consider creating your own categories for your budget.

Using a canned worksheet is a great place to start preparing your budget. Most of them contain enough categories to help you focus and to give you ideas of categories you might need to add.

Creating your own categories helps you include personal priorities in your budget. For example, if you attend a leather group or event on a regular basis, you'll want to include the dues or fees for those activities in your budget. Make sure to include categories for your hobbies and interests so you can budget funds to support them.

I will caution you not to develop too many categories. Doing so may be self-defeating since the purpose of a budget is to stick to it and having too much to track may prevent you from doing so for any length of time.
Once you've chosen a worksheet and included your own categories, it's time to collect your bills and pay stubs.

Calculating Amounts

With your pay stubs and other income paperwork collected, complete the income portion of your budget worksheet. You should calculate your gross income, i.e. the income you earn prior to taxes and other deductions. Those deductions will be removed in other areas of your budget.

Next, use your bills to complete the sections for housing, utilities and other recurring expenses. Don't forget things like loans and bills for which you do not receive paper bills. If you have bills that vary from month to month, average the amount based on three or four months of fees. Remember to take into account seasonal changes in bills as well. For example, the only thing in my home that runs on natural gas is my furnace. That means my natural gas bill is going to be significantly higher during the winter months than it is during the summer.

It is important to realistically assess projected spending in the areas of the budget where you may not have bills or receipts to demonstrate your actual spending. It is also a good idea to give yourself some buffer in these areas to account for emergencies and unexpected overages. Find a balance between your necessary spending and the cushion you need to have in order to be prepared for unforeseen expenses.

Once you've filled in the projected areas of your budget, it's time to start tracking your spending.

Recording Expenses

Now comes the hard part. Tracking your expenses can be time consuming and frustrating, but it is a necessary part of effective budgeting.

Find a method that works for you. I've found that keeping receipts for everything in a particular place in my wallet and then entering them into the form at the end of a week works well. You may also want to keep a small notebook to track any cash spending or spending that doesn't have a receipt.

It is important to maintain an accurate account not only of what you spend but where you spend it so that when you review your budget you can find areas of spending that can be adjusted. I'd be willing to be that after a week of tracking you'll be surprised where you spend your money.

Once you've entered all your expenditures, compare them to your projected amounts. How accurate were your estimates? Where do you need to make adjustments? Be sure to also compare your total expenditures to your total income. Positives are surpluses, negatives are shortfall.

Don't panic if you find areas of negatives. The next part of this activity will ask you to look at these areas and make changes.

Setting Goals and Making Adjustments

Now that you've entered your expenditures and compared them with your income, you should have a pretty good idea of where you spend your money. You should also have a good idea of where you might be able to make changes to meet your financial goals.

Perhaps you've seen that you spend $50 per month on coffee. If you're short in another area of your budget, cutting down on your coffee might be a good place to find the funds.

If you have a savings goal, whether for long-term savings or for a particular purchase, looking through your expenditures is a good way to find areas in which to cut back in order to meet those savings goals.

I strongly recommend that you commit to using your budget for not less than six months, with a substantive review of your spending at the end of each month. If you don't make budgeting and sticking to your budget a priority, you won't do it and you won't benefit from knowing where you spend your money.

I've included a single worksheet in this chapter for each of the first six months. The Submissive's Activity Book Companion contains a year's worth of budget worksheets. I hope you'll find them useful.

Budget Planner

Budget Planner

INCOME

AMOUNT	SOURCE	DATE

FIXED EXPENSES

BILL	DATE DUE	TOTAL

EVERYDAY EXPENSES

STORE	DATE	TOTAL

SAVINGS

PURPOSE	DATE	TOTAL

Shari A. Malin Copyright 2020

Expenses

Expenses

EXPENSE NAME	DATE	CATEGORY	BUSINESS	SPENT	TOTAL

Developing a Schedule

Developing a Working Schedule

Developing a Working Schedule

You may be asking yourself why I would include a section on creating a working schedule in a book designed for submissives. There are several reasons this chapter is important to your development as an efficient and effective submissive. In order to know for certain that you have the time to take on the monumental task of caring for someone else, you must first know what your own current obligations are. It is also important that you continue to progress toward any personal goals while you are engaged in a power exchange. Finally, you'll want to be able to say yes to pleasurable activities without fearing you'll be jeopardizing any of your goals or priorities. A schedule will help you with all of these things.

Getting Started

I recommend beginning the process of developing a working schedule by setting goals, both personal and leather. Choose the areas of your life in which you wish to set goals, Perhaps you have training and service goals. Maybe you have goals for your family and home, your finances and career, or your physical health. Whatever areas of your life you wish to improve, make a list so you can stay focused.

In each of the areas of your life, list the goals you wish to work toward. Each goal statement you make should meet the following criteria. Each statement should be specific, measurable, attainable, realistic, and timely*(Nikitina footnote).

When you write down your goals, be as specific as possible. Don't just say you want to learn new skills, list the new skills you want to learn.

In order to achieve a goal, you have to be able to measure your success. Perhaps you goal is to learn to set a formal table. Make sure to include a test of your success (such as hosting a formal dinner) to demonstrate mastery of your goal. Choosing criteria for success will help you make your goals measurable.

Goals should challenge you and require a strong commitment, but they should still be within the realm of possibility. The criteria you develop for the measurability of your goal will help you determine if your goal is attainable.

A goal should be realistic so that it is attainable. Set your goals high enough so it is satisfactory to meet them but keep in mind those things that simply cannot be done. If you know, for example, that it will take a year to reach an educational goal, setting it within a six month time frame is not realistic.

Be sure to create a clear target for achievement. If you don't give yourself a deadline, the goal is likely never to be attained.

As you write out your goals, be sure to use positive language. Stating what will be done, rather than what won't be done, makes goals more attainable. Be sure to include enough details to make the goal statement specific and which reflect the criteria you have set for measurability.

Finally, it is a good idea to set up rewards for yourself for attaining your goals. If you don't know what you're going to get out of reaching a goal, you're less likely to be motivated to work toward it.

After you've clearly stated your goals, you should prioritize them. Review your goals and decide which are most important to your overall goals of improvement. Prioritizing your goals will help you place them into your schedule and keep you moving toward them.

It is important to prioritize your responsibilities as well. When I first entered into a true 24/7 total power exchange relationship I found that my previous priorities of work, friends and family had to be changed. The only priority I had which could be shunted back was the part-time work I had been doing. I found that in order to give my full attention to the one I served, I had to give up three of the four jobs I worked.

It isn't always easy to make these kinds of decisions. When you look at your life and your goals, you are going to have to decide where your priorities lie. I know now that my priorities are focused more on family (both natural and leather) than they are on my work-a-holic tendencies. You will have to make those types of decisions for yourself. The only recommendation I can make to you is to take time to consider your priorities and recognize that they may change over time.

Making a Schedule

Now that you've clearly stated your goals and made your priorities clear, it's time to make your schedule. I'm going to recommend using monthly and weekly schedules along with to-do lists. The monthly calendars I've included in this book have space for goals, appointments, and to-do lists.

Annual Scheduling

I recommend going through each of the monthly calendars and adding the recurring events to them right at the beginning. This will help you to remember those annual events such as birthdays, anniversaries, and others.

Once you've listed all the annual events in your life, you can combine that list with a box or folder full of cards filed by month and event so you don't forget to recognize those annual events.

Weekly Planning Calendar

I've included a weekly focus calendar for each mont you can use to get your recurring weekly schedule in order. Paired with your monthly calendar, goals, and to-do, these calendars should be enough for you to continue to plan going forward.

Beginning with your weekly planning calendar helps you to enter your time requirements based on your priorities. You'll likely need to begin by entering your work times into the calendar. For example, my working schedule is actually very open. I rarely need be in a specific place at a specific time. Unless you have a job like mine, however, your work times are likely going to take up a significant portion of your weekly schedule.

You may also wish to schedule specific tasks into your work time. If you have assessable tasks to complete for work, make time for them in your weekly planner.

Once you have blocked off time for work, turn to your goal lists and review your priorities. You'll want to schedule in time to engage in the activities which move you toward your goals based on their priority rating. For example, one of my goals is to exercise in order to be healthy. It is a high priority goal for me for several reasons, including the order from the owner to take care of his property. As such, after work time, my work-out time is my next priority. Whatever your goals are, make certain to put them into your schedule so you can work toward meeting them.

Your next task is to schedule contingency time into your projects and priorities. You will find, through experience, that most projects take much more time than you expect them to. It is important to schedule time for fixing problems and extending deadlines so you don't become discouraged when your goals miss your deadlines. Remember that the more unpredictable your job or your goals are, the more contingency time you will need to schedule.

For example, my writing takes sometimes more and sometimes less time than I might plan. Some days I just can't find the groove and other days I know I can't stop writing or I'll lose the groove. I need to schedule my writing into my day so the owner knows what my obligations are but I also put a buffer around my writing time so that if I want or need more time, I have it.

After you have fit in all the time you need for work, goals, and other priorities, what you have left of your waking day is your "free" time. This is the time you have for meeting the expectations of an owner, for attending lifestyle events, for having fun. You may initially be disappointed to see how little time is left for you after your goals and priorities, but remember that you have chosen your priorities and you can always make adjustments. If there is a particular event you want to attend but it conflicts with another goal, you can decide which task has a higher priority. Sometimes these decisions are not easy. Often, we end up doing what is right for the long-run rather than what is fun for the short-term. However if you consider your goals priorities, losing out on a party in favor of a seminar that moves you toward a goal is the better choice.

Monthly Planning Calendar

Begin by transferring your annual events to the monthly planning calendar. Then enter the one-time events like conventions, munches, appointments, etc. into your calendar. Be sure to consult your weekly planning calendar to resolve any conflicts that might arise as you combine your weekly responsibilities with the one-time events and appointments which arise.

Periodic Review

Once you have developed your schedule, it is important to review it periodically to ensure it is working for you. You should also review your goals and priorities, making changes as you make progress. Periodic review of your schedule will allow you to find time you might put to better use or adjust your priorities to better meet your goals.

1

January

Monthly Notes

MONTH:

MONDAY	TUESDAY	WEDNESDAY	THURSDAY	FRIDAY	SATURDAY	SUNDAY
1						
2						
3						
4						
5						

February

Monthly Notes

MONTH:

MONDAY	TUESDAY	WEDNESDAY	THURSDAY	FRIDAY	SATURDAY	SUNDAY
1						
2						
3						
4						
5						

March

Monthly Notes

MONTH:

MONDAY	TUESDAY	WEDNESDAY	THURSDAY	FRIDAY	SATURDAY	SUNDAY
1						
2						
3						
4						
5						

April

Monthly Notes

MONTH:

MONDAY	TUESDAY	WEDNESDAY	THURSDAY	FRIDAY	SATURDAY	SUNDAY
1						
2						
3						
4						
5						

May

Monthly Notes

MONTH:

MONDAY	TUESDAY	WEDNESDAY	THURSDAY	FRIDAY	SATURDAY	SUNDAY
1						
2						
3						
4						
5						

June

Monthly Notes

MONTH:

MONDAY	TUESDAY	WEDNESDAY	THURSDAY	FRIDAY	SATURDAY	SUNDAY

July

Monthly Notes

MONTH:

MONDAY	TUESDAY	WEDNESDAY	THURSDAY	FRIDAY	SATURDAY	SUNDAY
1						
2						
3						
4						
5						

August

Monthly Notes

MONTH:

MONDAY	TUESDAY	WEDNESDAY	THURSDAY	FRIDAY	SATURDAY	SUNDAY
1						
2						
3						
4						
5						

September

Monthly Notes

MONTH:

MONDAY	TUESDAY	WEDNESDAY	THURSDAY	FRIDAY	SATURDAY	SUNDAY
1						
2						
3						
4						
5						

October

Monthly Notes

MONTH:

MONDAY	TUESDAY	WEDNESDAY	THURSDAY	FRIDAY	SATURDAY	SUNDAY
1						
2						
3						
4						
5						

November

Monthly Notes

MONTH:

MONDAY	TUESDAY	WEDNESDAY	THURSDAY	FRIDAY	SATURDAY	SUNDAY
1						
2						
3						
4						
5						

Shari A. Malin Copyright 2020

December

Monthly Notes

MONTH:

MONDAY	TUESDAY	WEDNESDAY	THURSDAY	FRIDAY	SATURDAY	SUNDAY
1						
2						
3						
4						
5						

Monthly Calendars

January

January

MONDAY	TUESDAY	WEDNESDAY	THURSDAY	FRIDAY	SATURDAY	SUNDAY

Goals and Things to do

February

February

MONDAY	TUESDAY	WEDNESDAY	THURSDAY	FRIDAY	SATURDAY	SUNDAY

Goals and Things to do

March

March

MONDAY	TUESDAY	WEDNESDAY	THURSDAY	FRIDAY	SATURDAY	SUNDAY

Goals and Things to do

April

April

MONDAY	TUESDAY	WEDNESDAY	THURSDAY	FRIDAY	SATURDAY	SUNDAY

Goals and Things to do

May

May

MONDAY	TUESDAY	WEDNESDAY	THURSDAY	FRIDAY	SATURDAY	SUNDAY

Goals and Things to do

June

June

MONDAY	TUESDAY	WEDNESDAY	THURSDAY	FRIDAY	SATURDAY	SUNDAY

Goals and Things to do

July

July

MONDAY	TUESDAY	WEDNESDAY	THURSDAY	FRIDAY	SATURDAY	SUNDAY

Goals and Things to do

August

August

MONDAY	TUESDAY	WEDNESDAY	THURSDAY	FRIDAY	SATURDAY	SUNDAY

Goals and Things to do

September

September

MONDAY	TUESDAY	WEDNESDAY	THURSDAY	FRIDAY	SATURDAY	SUNDAY

Goals and Things to do

October

October

MONDAY	TUESDAY	WEDNESDAY	THURSDAY	FRIDAY	SATURDAY	SUNDAY

Goals and Things to do

November

November

MONDAY	TUESDAY	WEDNESDAY	THURSDAY	FRIDAY	SATURDAY	SUNDAY

Goals and Things to do

December

December

MONDAY	TUESDAY	WEDNESDAY	THURSDAY	FRIDAY	SATURDAY	SUNDAY

Goals and Things to do

Printed in Great Britain
by Amazon